Printed by Pickards.org.uk

Unit 1, 104 Fitzwalter Road, Sheffield S2 2SP

Telephone 0114 275 7222

www.youbooks.co.uk

J R Wrigley, one of Sheffield most prolific authors, has also produced Ten Camera A5 books showing over 1000 different images of the City of Sheffield.
He has also produced t'owd locals an A5 book on Sheffield public houses which have long since disappeared from the city's landscape.
Wrigley's Sheffield is a larger A4 book with many more unseen images of Sheffield.

Introduction

The 1970s are slipping back into memory. And a good thing too you may think. Electricity was rationed due to a miners' strike leading to a three-day week for many workers; Britain had to go cap in hand to the International Monetary Fund for a loan to bail us out; Prime Minister Callaghan sang for us through the Winter of Discontent when rubbish piled in the streets and the dead lay unburied. We were all coming to terms with the new decimal currency.

In Sheffield high-rise flats were the order of the day while perfectly good houses were demolished. A good slice was carved off the much-loved Peace Gardens to make way for new extensions to the Town Hall - disrespectfully christened 'the Egg Box' by sceptical Sheffielders. It was the age of the bus. Trams had disappeared and as yet there was no Supertram.

It was also the age of work. British rail ran the railways, the English Steel Corporation was nationalised, most of the steel works were active, small shops thrived because supermarkets were only just beginning to arrive. Motors there were but nothing like the numbers today. You could get on a bus that went right across town - up Waingate, Haymarket, High Street, Fargate, Pinstone Street, The Moor and you could stop the bus almost outside the shop you were visiting.

Pedestrisnisation began in the 1970s - first Fargate, then The Moor - also Exchange Street and Dixon Lane. Arundel Gate had been created in the 1960s but most of the huge buildings we now see had not arrived.

Many well-remembered shops were still to be seen since the multi-nationals had not put them out of business -Wilson Pecks, Redgates, Woolworths, Timpsons, Cole Brothers, Proctors, Bradleys, Wigfalls, Prestons, Hartley Seeds, Barney Goodman, Ward's bookshop, Cann - the Music Man and so many more.

Still we had the Castle Square Underpass. Again Sheffielders had a name for it - 'Hole in the Road'. and I know some who have searched without success for photos of the aquarium remembering it as a favourite meeting place.

If some of these photos stir memories that is what photos are for. Years ago a lucky prize-winner won with the phrase: "Click went the camera and - we smiled years later." I hope these bring a smile.

Index

Sheaf Market - Entrance from Broad Street. When this was taken in 1972 this open market had short time to go. It was cleared in 1973 and the area became a car park.

An unusual shot of the escalators to the Hole in the Road. On this particular day they were working which was not always the case. 9th June 1974.

Orchard Street with three well-remembered venues: Sunshine Health shop - left; the Raincoat Shop and beyond the Orchard Cafe. 3rd May 1975.

Pinstone Street: Blind matchseller outside Cambridge Arcade. 3rd May 1975.

Boots Corner. The dark building was once known as Forster's Building in Edwardian times. 18th July 1974.

In the forground Penistone Road with Rutland Road left and Bedford Street
to the right Bury's Globe Works and beyond Industrial Sheffield.

High Street - Going down to the Hole-in-the Road. 1975

Two panoramic views of High Street taken 20th July 1974

Mary Street was an industrial street between Hereford Street and Shoreham Street. 1975

Middlewood Hospital as it was in the late 1970s. Much of this area is now a new housing estate.

Top: A view of Woodseats taken from Chesterfield Road.
Bottom: Hoyle Street factory. Both images 1970s.

Pinstone Street on a wet day in June showing the tram sheds (later bus sheds) that survived until around 1985.

A view of Ecclesall Road at its junction with London Road before development. There is a good view of Sunwin House, home of the Sheffield & Ecclesall Co-op before it was demolished. c1972

TWIN TOWERS

This is an unusual view of the twin cooling towers and of Blackburn Meadows Power Station which they served.
I was down on the bank of the Tinsley Canal looking towards the Tinsley Viaduct.
The power station was demolished some time ago but the towers survived - a landmark to drivers using the M1 Motorway and they became an icon to the people of Sheffield.
Last year they were declared unsafe and - amid protests - were removed (2010).
This photograph was taken on 5th May 1974.

This part of Surrey Street has undergone two changes since I took this image in 1970. Firstly it was replaced by the Egg Box and when that was demolished the Winter Gardens and the Hotel took its place.

A panoramic view of Angel Street in the 1970s. I do not have the exact date for this one taken with a Russian Horizont camera that sometimes worked well but sometimes didn't.

Taken on the Wicker around 1972 this shows the buildings that would be demolished to make way for the new Derek Dooley Way - part of the Ring Road.

West Bar roundabout looking down Corporation Street. This has now all gone. 16th June 1974

A view of Sheaf Square taken around Christmas time 1976

The corner of Surrey Street and Norfolk Street photographed in June 1974. Hibberd's Art Shop always had an interesting display. Sheffield Savings Bank was still handling money. The Pizza Parlour was starting a trend for Italian food.

As the development of Park Square got under way these two were getting out. Ever since the 1950s I cannot remember a time when something wasn't going or coming. This image was taken on 7th July 1974.

What more is there to say except this was a jam packed High Street twenty years before Supertram.
Taken on 9th June 1974.

When the Sheaf Market was open Dixon Lane was busy, mostly with greengrocers.
This stall was outside King's grocers - note their prices for 1973.

Following the closure of the open market this covered part of the Sheaf Market remained open for a little while longer and is shown here in 1973. The Patnick name was king in junk at this time.

High Street below Boots showing the short-lived underpass that became redundant when Fargate was pedestrianised. The date was 18th July 1974.

A 1977 view of Arundel Gate at Howard Street. St. Mary's Church and the Furnival Square overpass can be seen in the distance. It puzzles me that we have so many circular Squares in Sheffield. .

Bridge Street - a much-used bus terminus in 1974.

The ABC Cinema viewed from the window of Castle House on Angel Street. 25th May 1974

Castlegate (left) and Blonk Street. A tower block now occupies the centre. The urinal probably discarded its effluent into the River Don.

The Canal Basin in its working days. 7th July 1974

Two very different images of Castle Square as it was in 1974.
On the left a view of the roundabout taken in May and on the right two ladies out on a shopping trip.

Proctors Furniture Store stood next to Cole Brothers but when that shop moved Proctors soon disappeared. Proctors stood at Nos. 20-26. Fargate The date was May 1975.

Haymarket footbridge joining King Street to the upper floors of British Home Stores 1975.
It was possible to walk from King Street along Haymarket to Exchange Street by using this footbridge.

Cornish Street, Cornish Works May 1974

Fitzalan Square viewed from C&A Modes. May 1975.

Infirmary Road looking towards Hoyle Street. The Roscoe cinema/bingo hall and all the surrounding area disappeared to accomodate Supertram in the 1990s. This image was taken on 16th June 1974,

Hill Street - off London Road 8th May 1974. John Collins is the name on the dray but where's the horse?

The City Hall and Holly Street with Andrews' School Shop and the CWS Shirt Factory in the distance. 29th July 1974.

London Road looking south. 27th July 1974

The Moor underpass has recently been filled in.
This photo from 1979 shows it when it was still much in use.

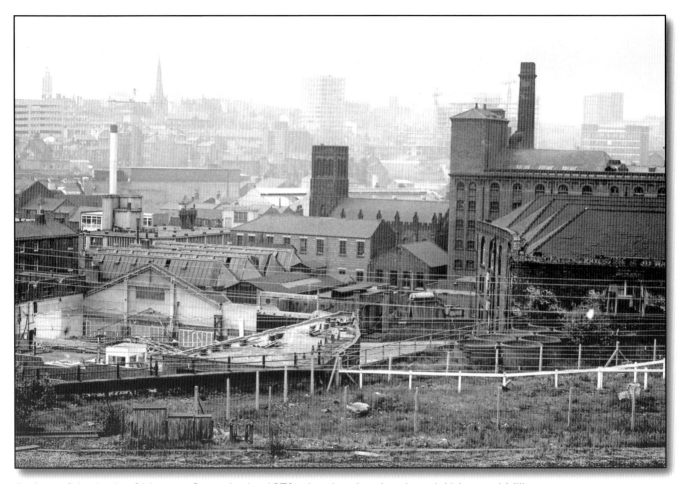

A view of the back of Nursery Street in the 1970s showing the church and Aizlewood Mill.

The bottom of The Moor was still largely undeveloped when this was taken in 1975

Penistone Road meets Infirmary Road where Shalesmoor begins. May 1975

The old Peace Gardens. Possibly old-fashioned but very well tended. This is how it looked in 1975.

Redgates was Sheffield's leading toy retailer until it was overtaken by a new multi-national consortium. This shows it in its heyday. 3rd May 1975

The London Road salerooms of T.C. Harrison's motors. Note the prices of what were virtually new cars to see what inflation has done since this was taken on 27th July 1974.

Haymarket balcony. This walkway was closed some years ago. Probably because of parents who let their children play precariously on them. Image taken 9th June 1975.

West Bar Green. The building on the right was first a police station - then a fire station and now serves as a fire service museum. The tall building is the new police station due to be demolished shortly. Photo date 1972.

The Shude Hill side of the Sheaf Market in 1972

Two pubs on Charles Street. The Phoenix went a long time ago but the Roebuck Tavern has survived although now surrounded by high rise buildings. Taken in 1972.

Fargate 3rd May 1975 following pedestrianisation.

The Raven was later named the Hornblower and then to O'Hagans or something similar.
Everything here was demolished including Kenning's Parts Centre. Top of Fitzwilliam Street. Taken 26th July 1974

The date was 26th July 1974 when this delivery of new cars was made to Kenning's Car Hire on West Street.

Jessop Hospital, Leavygreave Road 1977

Whether the road takes its name from the Lansdowne Hotel or vice versa - in either case Lansdowne Road has now gone for ever. 27th May 1974.

Netherthorpe roundabout looking down Broad Lane with a good view of the Jessop Hospital and its extensions. 19th July 1974

Osborne's Clyde Works are seen here on Blonk Street. They occupied much of that street with offices on the Wicker. To the right is what was then the Royal Victoria Hotel.

The 1977 Star Walk. These cheerful walkers are passing the historic Travellers Inn at Wadsley Bridge.
I have learnt that the Travellers Inn is now to be demolished.

Pinstone Street at the Peace Gardens showing the Town Hall extensions nearing completion. 3rd May 1975

Shude Hill with Commercial Street to the left. The building to the right has been replaced with a modern hotel. 9th June 1975.

Surrey Street when the 'Egg Box' was just being built. 1974

Tudor Street shown here was swallowed up by the new Tudor Square. The site for the new Town Hall extension is boarded up and the east side of the Town Hall would soon be a memory. The date was June 1974.

Union Street, 3rd May 1975. The Victorian building had to go.

Haymarket to Waingate 1975

This walkway ran under Arundel Gate from Howard Street. The Fiesta night club is to be seen. 1975

Union Street as it was in 1970. The shops were awaiting demolition and the small white building which belonged to Brook Shaw - the Ford car dealers - would soon disappear.

West Bar Green. These shops will be remembered by older viewers. 1972

Overlooking the railway line this is land between the Wicker and Nursery Street. The dark buildin was on Andrew Street and in the very centre can be seen the historic Bull and Oak pub. 17th June 1974.

Campo Lane Bus Terminus 1975. This terminus had a short life.

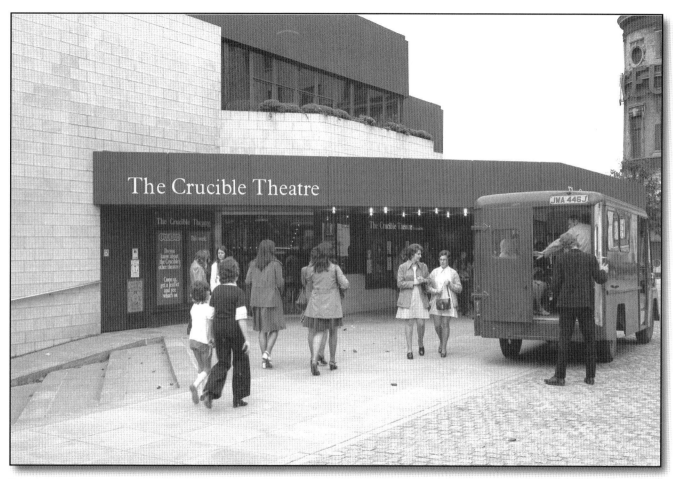

Early days at The Crucible Theatre 18th July 1974

London Road. 15th June 1974

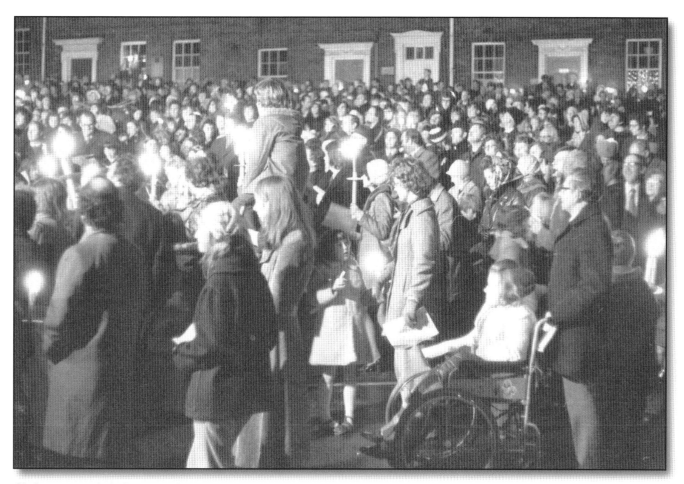

Christmas carols in Paradise Square. Arranged by Radio Sheffield. I don't recall that this experiment was ever repeated nor ever since has there been such a gathering in the square.

The rose bed in the foreground was the graveyard of St. Philip's Church. Just to the left of centre is the Bury's Glove Works and the pub is the Royal Lancer which was situated on Penistone Road. Taken in May 1974.

The date was 20th July 1974 when I snapped these young people queueing outside Top Rank on Arundel Gate.

Forge Dam is typical of the many dams that are to be found in Sheffield valleys - once used to turn the mill wheels. The mills have long gone but the dams remain - now used by fishermen. This was taken on May 10th 1975.

Western Bank. Amateur artists' paintings offered for sale.
10th May 1975.

Addy Street 8th May 1974

The approach to Castle Square Underpass was either by an escalator (shown here reflected in the window) or by a ramp. It was built in the days when traffic was king and pedestrians were forced underground. Taken 9th June 1974.

The Cathedral Forecourt showing two well remembered businesses - Henry Spencer & Sons, Auctioneers and Estate Agents and Eadon, Lockwood & Riddle - auctioneers. July 1974.

St. Mary's Gate under construction. 27th July 1974

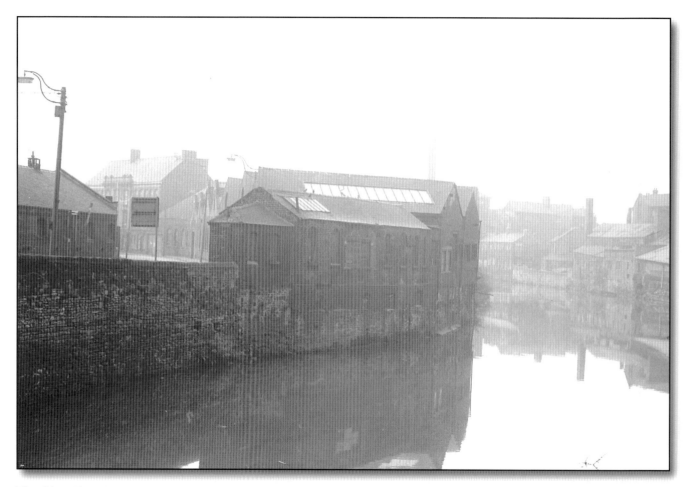

The River Don looking upstream from Rutland Road bridge. The date was 16th June 1974

The magnificent Victorian Education Offices on Leopold Street as they were when in use. They were attached to the Central School. Partly gutted they are now in use for a variety of retail purposes. At least the facade has been retained. This image was taken July 1974.

London Road: 53-67 T.C. Harrison's car sales; 75 The Albion pub; 79 Ron Harrison's camera shop;
81 Mrs; Minott - jeweller; 83 Sewing Machine Centre. 28th July 1974.

Broomhall Flats 27th July 1974 - later demolished.

Orchard Street. 3rd May 1975 with the Grand Hotel undergoing demolition. 3rd May 1975.

On 3rd May 1975 an Antiques Fair was held in the Cutler's Hall. I don't think there has been another one since.

This fine building has stood on Cross Burgess Street throughout my life but a few years ago was sold by the Army. I fear it may be demolished. The date is May 1974

The Moor before pedestrianisation. This couple are going down the tunnel that took them safely across Furnival Gate. May 1974..

Silver Street Head viewed from West Bar Green. On the right the Tenter Street tram sheds (later buses) are being demolished. Date: 1972.

West Bar viewed from West Bar Green. The filling station on the right was on the site of the old Surrey Music Hall which burnt down in 1865. I have a postcard drawing depicting it ablaze published by J.W. Mottershaw.

Notes

Notes